Sharks

Children's Nature Library

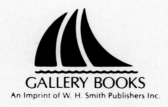

GALLERY BOOKS
An Imprint of W. H. Smith Publishers Inc.

Louis Weber, C.E.O.
Publications International, Ltd.
7373 North Cicero Avenue
Lincolnwood, Illinois 60646

ISBN 0-8317-6473-2

This edition published in 1991 by Gallery Books, an imprint of W.H. Smith Publishers, Inc., 112 Madison Avenue, New York, New York 10016.

Gallery Books are available for bulk purchase for sales and promotions and premium use. For details write or telephone the Manager of Special Sales, W.H. Smith Publishers, Inc., 112 Madison Avenue, New York, New York 10016; (212) 532-6600.

Written by Eileen Spinelli

Credits:
Animals/Animals: Ashod Frances: 19; Mickey Gibson: 24; Zig Leszczynski: 42, 58; Oxford Scientific Films: Tony Crabtree: 51; R. Ingo Riepl: 27, 29; Carl Roessler: 23, 30, 34, 36, 38, 53; James D. Watt: 10, 62; Fred Whitehead: 6, 15; **Tom Campbell:** 50, 54, 57; **Ellis Wildlife Collection:** Gary Bell: 10, 20, 26, 52; Richard Herrmann: 40; **FPG International:** Kenneth Garrett: 25; John C. Gorman: Front Cover, 1, 28; H. Hall: 24; Carl Roessler: 6, 37, Back Cover; **Alex Kerstitch:** 18, 56; **Nicklin & Associates:** Flip Nicklin: 7, 8, 13, 16, 22, 54, 63; © **1990 Sea World, Inc.:** Reproduced by permission. All rights reserved.: Jerry Roberts: 4, 55; Sea World Photo: 12, 42; **Marty Snyderman:** 3, 9, 11, 14, 16, 17, 21, 22, 26, 30, 31, 32, 33, 35, 39, 44, 45, 46, 48, 49, 56, 59, 60, 61, 62, 64; **Tom Stack & Associates:** Jeff Foott: 12; **Tyrell Museum:** Vladimir Krb: 5; **Doug Wechsler:** 16; **Norbert Wu:** 8, 40, 41, 43, 46, 47.

Table of Contents

The History
of Sharks

Sharks have been swimming in our oceans for millions and millions of years. They were alive when dinosaurs ruled the earth. Only a few animals have been around for that long. Sharks have changed very little in all that time.

Since early times, people have been afraid of sharks. Our ancestors often thought of them as sea monsters. Some people from South Pacific islands worshiped sharks as gods. They believed shark-gods ruled the earth from underwater caves. In 1872, the HMS *Challenger* set sail to study sharks and other sea creatures and plants. This trip started the science of oceanography.

The History of Sharks

Today, we understand sharks much better than our ancestors did. Scientists have learned a great deal by studying sharks in aquariums and in the open sea. There are over 300 different kinds of sharks known, and there are probably more that haven't been discovered yet. Sharks are one of the oldest fish, and they are one of the smartest. Many people still think that all sharks are ferocious man-eaters. Actually, only a very few kinds of sharks will ever attack people, and even they won't do so very often. Still, sharks can be dangerous, and it's important to be careful whenever one is around.

Shark Sizes

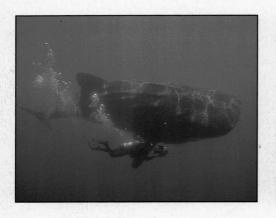 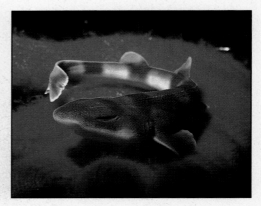

Sharks come in all different sizes. Some sharks are as big as whales and weigh several thousand pounds. The average shark, though, is smaller than a full-grown person, and some are even smaller than babies. A full-grown cigar shark could rest comfortably in the palm of your hand. Of course, you might want to wear gloves.

Where Sharks Live

Almost every sea in the world has sharks. Some sharks live in the open ocean, far from land. Some, like the nurse shark, live near the shore. Coral reefs are home to many sharks. Others look for cozy underwater caves or burrow into muddy seabeds. Many sharks like warm water, and there are some that travel with the warm ocean currents. But the sleeper shark swims in icy polar seas.

Baby Sharks

A baby shark is called a pup. All shark pups come from eggs. Some mothers keep the eggs inside their bodies until they hatch, and the pups are born live. Others make egg cases, sometimes called "mermaids' purses," that attach to plants on the seafloor. The horn shark lays screw-shaped egg cases and twists them into cracks and crevices in rocks. Sand tiger sharks have one pup at a time. Sevengill sharks can have over 100 at once. Shark pups usually look just like their parents, and they must take care of themselves from the minute they are born.

Shark Senses

The shark has an incredible sense of smell. It is often called the "swimming nose." Sharks can smell odors over a mile away. They can also hear sounds that humans can't. Humans have five senses—taste, smell, sight, hearing, and touch. Sharks have a sixth sense located in special pores on their heads. These pores sense electric currents given off by other sea creatures. It is possible that sharks also use these pores to navigate by sensing the earth's magnetic fields—the pores would tell them where the North Pole is, much like a compass does for us.

Shark Senses

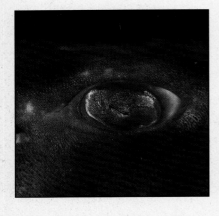

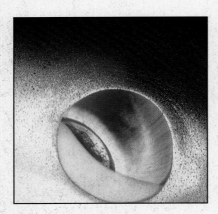

People used to think sharks had poor eyesight. Actually, some sharks can see better in the dark than we can. Some sharks have tiny eyes. Other sharks' eyes are big. Sharks who feed at night have catlike eyes—they shine in the dark.

A shark's keen senses are very important in helping it find food. One of the reasons sharks are such great hunters is that they can detect and home in on animals that are far away or well hidden.

Sharks & Breathing

The shark does not breathe through its nose. Its nose is just for smelling. A shark breathes with its gills. As it swims, water flows through the gills, and the gills take oxygen from the water. Most sharks have to swim constantly in order to breathe. Unlike other fish, they are not able to pump water through their mouths and over their gills. Some, however, can breathe just fine lying on the bottom of the sea. No one knows why some kinds of sharks are able to do this and others are not.

Shark Teeth

The teeth of some ancient sharks were the size of a man's hand. Today even the biggest shark teeth are no more than two inches long. Different sharks have different shapes of teeth, depending on the kind of food they eat. Some are like triangles. The sand tiger shark's teeth are long, pointed spikes. The teeth of the swellshark look like small tacks. Sharks that eat shellfish have small, crushing teeth for breaking through the hard shells of their prey.

Shark Teeth

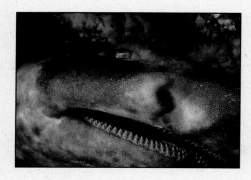

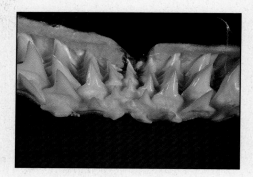

Most sharks have loose teeth. Teeth can fall out with every bite. But don't call the dentist! Sharks have rows and rows of replacement teeth. When one tooth falls out, another moves up to take its place. Usually, each new tooth is just a bit bigger than the one it replaces, so a shark's teeth are always getting larger. A typical shark probably goes through thousands and thousands of teeth in its lifetime.

The Eating Machine

Sharks are built to do one thing: Eat! People sometimes call the shark "the eating machine." Some sharks eat large fish, stingrays, turtles, or seals. Others slurp up plankton, which is a "sea soup" of plants, fish eggs, shrimp, and tiny crabs. Sharks will also swallow unusual things like tools, raincoats, boat cushions, and soup kettles.

The Eating Machine

Some sharks feed at night, and others eat during the day. The spinner shark spins up through its dinner of fish. The sand shark swallows its food whole. Blood in the water can drive some sharks into a "feeding frenzy." Sharks from all over race to the scene, snapping at anything in reach—including each other.

Danger!

Most sharks are not dangerous to people. Some, like the basking shark, are quite peaceful. Most others try to avoid people as much as they can. Even some of the fiercest sharks will not attack unless they are teased or threatened. But there are some that will attack for no reason, and when they do, they can be deadly. The great white, the bull shark, the blue shark, the hammerhead, and the mako are all known to have attacked people.

Danger!

In order to learn more about sharks and how they live, scientists and photographers study sharks in the ocean. They watch from safe steel cages. Some even swim with the sharks. Experienced divers have been known to touch sharks, and sometimes they even feed them. Of course, they are always *very* careful.

Mako

Makos are fighters. If a mako is hooked on a
fishing line, it will put up a great struggle. It will
leap high into the air. Unlike most sharks, the
mako is warm-bodied. Its body is specially
designed to hold in heat, so that its temperature
is usually a few degrees warmer than the water it
swims in. Warm muscles help it swim faster than
any other shark. The mako's deep blue color
makes it one of the most beautiful sharks. Makos
are found in warm waters away from the shore.
They feed mostly on large fish, especially tuna
and bluefish.

Great White Shark

The great white shark is always ready to eat. It will eat almost anything it can catch. It will even attack small boats. Its favorite food seems to be large marine mammals, like seals, porpoises, and sea lions, but it will also eat other sharks, fish, and even whales. The teeth of the great white are as sharp as razors and as hard as steel. Its triangle-shaped two-inch teeth are the largest of any shark.

Great White Shark

The great white is one of the largest sharks. It can grow to be over 20 feet long and weigh several thousand pounds. Some experts think that these sharks may get to be almost 30 feet long, but no great white of that size has ever been seen. Its huge size and deadly teeth make the great white one of the fiercest creatures in the ocean.

Great White Shark

The great white was named for its belly, which is as white as snow. Like the mako, it is warm-bodied, so it can swim fast and far. It sometimes leaps out of the water. Great whites prefer cool, temperate seas. They spend most of their time close to land, but some have been seen far out at sea. They are one of the few sharks that will attack people.

Angelshark

The angelshark is a smooth and graceful swimmer that can grow to be about five or six feet long. It has a wide, flat body and four large fins that look a little like an angel's wings. This shark spends much of its time lying on the seafloor and waiting for a meal to swim by. It is usually found in temperate and tropical waters near the shore.

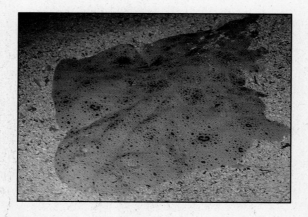

Bull Shark

You don't have to go to the ocean to find a bull shark. It is the only shark that spends much of its time in lakes and rivers. The bull shark prowls in shallow water, feeding on whatever it can find. It will eat just about anything—even other sharks. The bull shark is large and heavy, but it's a fast swimmer.

Blue Shark

The blue shark is quite a traveler. It spends almost all of its time far out in the ocean, swimming from one place to another. One blue shark is known to have traveled almost 6,000 miles in a little over one year. Blues are also known to swim at many different depths. They can often be found near the surface, but they probably dive as far as 1,000 feet below the surface several times a day as they search for food.

Blue Shark

You can usually identify a blue shark by its long flat snout, its huge jet-black eyes, and its unusual metallic blue color.

Blues can get to be very large (about 15 feet), and they don't seem to be afraid of people, as most sharks are. This means that they can be very dangerous. Fortunately, blues like deep water, and they never come near the shore.

Blue Shark

Blue sharks usually eat large fish, but they also like to take their meals from the huge schools of squid they sometimes find far out at sea. Whale hunters think of blue sharks as enemies because they will often feed on the hunters' catches before they are able to remove them from the water.

Basking Shark

The basking shark is a plankton-eater that sometimes grows to over 40 feet. It has very large gills that are used to strain microscopic plants and animals from ocean water. The basking shark is found in cold, deep northern waters. It spends much of its time near the surface, as if it were "basking" in the sun. Basking sharks are rarely seen during the winter. Scientists think that when the weather turns cold, they may swim to the ocean floor and hibernate.

Wobbegong

Another name for the wobbegong shark is the carpetshark. That's because it spends much of its time lying on the bottom looking like a lumpy, fringed carpet. The wobbegong is good at hiding. It has spots and colors that make it look like it's part of the seafloor. It also has fringe around its face. Sometimes a sea creature will swim up and nibble on its shaggy beard. The wobbegong nibbles right back with its daggerlike teeth. The wobbegong lives in warm water. Unlike most sharks, it never travels far from where it was born.

Swellshark

If it's disturbed, the swellshark does a swell trick. The three-foot-long fish gulps enough air or water to puff itself up like a balloon. This sudden increase in size can scare predators away, or it can lodge the swellshark in a group of rocks so that it can't be pulled out. During the day, the swellshark rests at the bottom of the sea. Sometimes a few swellsharks will nap together in a cozy heap. At night, the swellshark hunts for food. Its favorites are shrimp and lobster.

Hammerhead

One look at a hammerhead shark and you'll know how it got its name. One eye and one nostril sit at each end of the "hammer." Nobody knows why this shark has such a strange-looking head. Some experts think it may help the shark steer while it swims. Others think the shape makes the hammerhead a better hunter.

Hammerhead

Hammerheads are always found in coastal areas where the water is not very deep. Sometimes they are seen in only four or five feet of water. Like many sharks, they also seem to like warm, tropical seas rather than cooler waters. Some types of hammerheads migrate, moving north in the summer and south in the winter.

Hammerhead

The hammerhead is one of the only sharks that gathers in large groups called schools. The sharks all swim in the same direction, stay the same distance from each other, and turn in the same direction at the same time. Not long ago, thousands of them could be found in one school. But many, many hammerheads have been hunted by people for sport. Now, even the largest schools have only a few hundred hammerheads.

Whale Shark

The biggest fish in the world is the whale shark. Its teeth are small, but there are plenty of them. The mouth of the whale shark opens to six feet or more. The whale shark is a friendly, peaceful plankton-eater. Some experienced divers have even hitched rides on the back of this gentle creature.